"Rod McKuen is a romantic, an unabashed, totally committed romantic. Yet he has an understandable warmth and a virile intimacy that seem to reach out and stroke each of us into willing submission."

—*The New York Times*

". . . a man who has not only understood freedom for himself but for all the others for whom he writes and sings. The result is honesty—not just of his poetry, but of the man."

—*Los Angeles Herald Examiner*

"If you miss Rod McKuen's poetry, you're the poorer for it. He is one of the great poets of his or any country."

—*The Times*, London

"Rod McKuen's poetry is the most naked and unashamedly intimate verse I have ever read. Reading his work could be like reading the secret heart and soul of America itself."

—Aram Saroyan, *The Los Angeles Times*

"Rod McKuen writes love letters that often go astray. I am happy to say that many of them have found their way to me."

—W. H. Auden

A Biplane Book

Rod McKuen
Watch for the Wind

PUBLISHED BY POCKET BOOKS NEW YORK

A Biplane Book

Another *Original* publication of POCKET BOOKS

POCKET BOOKS, a Simon & Schuster division of
GULF & WESTERN CORPORATION
1230 Avenue of the Americas, New York, N.Y. 10020
BIPLANE BOOKS, P.O. Box 2783,
Hollywood, CA 90028

Cover photograph by Martin Lloyd

Photographs by Hy Fujita, Wayne Massie, Rod McKuen, Wade
Alexander, Donald Bradburn, Edward Habib McKuen, Alan
Catt, Helen Miljakovich, Peter Gottmer, Ben Spiegel, Bob
Lewis, Fred Neidner, David Nutter, and courtesy of William
Harris, Bob Crewe, and the Australian News Service

DESIGN: JACQUES CHAZAUD

ISBN: 0-671-43616-3

First Pocket Books printing February, 1983

10 9 8 7 6 5 4 3 2 1

BY ROD McKUEN

BOOKS

Prose
Finding My Father
An Outstretched Hand
A Book of Days

Poetry
And Autumn Came
Stanyan Street & Other Sorrows
Listen to the Warm
Lonesome Cities
In Someone's Shadow
Caught in the Quiet
Fields of Wonder
And to Each Season
Come to Me in Silence
Moment to Moment
Celebrations of the Heart
Beyond the Boardwalk
The Sea Around Me
Coming Close to the Earth
We Touch the Sky
The Power Bright and Shining
The Beautiful Strangers
Solitude's My Home (Fall 1983)

Collected Poems
Twelve Years of Christmas
A Man Alone
With Love
The Carols of Christmas
Seasons in the Sun
Alone
*The Rod McKuen Omnibus
Hand in Hand
Love's Been Good to Me
Looking for a Friend
Too Many Midnights
Watch for the Wind
*The Works of Rod McKuen

Music Collections
The McKuen/Sinatra Songbook
New Ballads
At Carnegie Hall
McKuen/Brel: Collaboration
28 Greatest Hits
Jean and Other Nice Things
McKuen Country
Through European Windows
Greatest Hits, Vol. I
Songs of Rod McKuen, Vol. I
Songs of Rod McKuen, Vol. II
Greatest Hits, Vol. II
Greatest Hits, Vol. III   *Available only in Great Britain

MAJOR FILM SCORES

The Prime of Miss Jean Brodie
A Boy Named Charlie Brown
Joanna
The Unknown War
Disney's Scandalous John
The Borrowers
Lisa Bright and Dark
Emily
Steinbeck's Travels with Charley
Come to Your Senses

CLASSICAL MUSIC

Ballet
Americana R.F.D.
Point/Counterpoint
Seven Elizabethan Dances
The Minotaur (Man to Himself)
Volga Song
Full Circle
The Plains of My Country
Dance Your Ass Off
The Man Who Tracked the Stars

Opera
The Black Eagle

Concertos
For Piano & Orchestra
For Cello & Orchestra
For Orchestra & Voice
For Guitar & Orchestra
#2 for Piano & Orchestra
For Four Harpsichords
Seascapes for Piano
Concerto for Orchestra

Symphonies, Symphonic Suites, Etc.
Symphony No. 1
Symphony No. 2
Ballad of Distances
The City
Symphony No. 3
Symphony No. 4
4 Quartets for Piano & Strings
4 Trios for Piano & Strings
Adagio for Harp & Strings
Rigadoon for Orchestra

This is a book for
Eve Kronfeld . . . because

Author's Note

Love is seldom carried by the wind—and life, less so. What the wind is best at is rearranging seasons, cycles, weather coming, weather already here. Though wind can be a part of weather and its make-up, it is always more. As the sun is not merely the chief property of a sunny or sunless day, but stays with us always—seen or unseen—so too the wind remains.

Few winds are cosmic, truly large enough to change each life for ill or good—capriciously or to suit a special need to themselves. Even flags, windchimes, and windmills could attest to that. Most winds, unless they tie up with a hurricane or travel with tornadoes, are personal by nature. As rain is nearly always regional, winds most often have their starting place just out of sight . . . around the corner, down the block.

I have loved the wind—when it brought blooms and blossoms, smells through an open window, when it changed the rain's direction, when I caught it on the quietest of days rearranging and playing with a crowd of clouds . . . when it caused tall trees to rustle in their highest branches and shower colored leaves upon a still green lawn to signal summer and then picked up a single sheet of paper and carried it in an arc across the sky like some magic carpet with a destination every bit as definite as a course set by Aladdin.

As I ballooned the Valley of a Thousand Hills, setting down in black villages where magic still surrounded such an apparition coming from the sky, or traveled up above the California meadows topping trees and skimming lakes, I must have known the wind would always care for me. However playful it became to shove and push my craft off-course or on some mornings stubbornly refused to help me move at all, it was a comfort knowing the wind was there.

So, long ago the wind and I, we made a truce, to not look forward or look back on what we might have each done to offend the other. It must have started when that first kite I went running with got tangled on a wire. I didn't curse the gust of wind that wound it there any more than I blamed lightning for a charred and burning fence it lit a match to or cursed the blue-white shaft that struck and halved a favorite tree.

No. While winter winds and those of other seasons still surprise me, I like surprises. The wind is an advantage and not an adversary. It clears and cleans more often than it heaps up havoc, and sweeps the dust away more often than it leaves it.

Parallel we go our ways, the winds and me and when we cross each other's path or course, we do so with a nod of courtesy.

I toast the wind. A giant—gentle, given half a chance. I have seen wind bring life and stir it. And love, that mystery of all mysteries, has floated and flowered for me, hatched by a single seed or puff of pollen that arrived by wisps of air so slight that none but me would know the courier that carried it was wind.

The wind of want. The wind of worry. The wind of change. All winds are friendly to the sailor in me, the soldier too, and I term every breeze a lovewind.

R.M.
June 1982, N.Y.

Contents

Being Warm Again

Unprepared for Autumn

The Confirmation of Colors

For FAROL SERETEAN

Spring never asks for anything. It knows its
strength—in ground made ready for the plow by
rain or winter's melted snow. One special day,
the color of the sunset spreads, reddens, grows
stronger. It seems to be a confirmation of
spring—even stronger than the pussy willow
branch. Spring colors, in the rural garden, com-
plement the sunset and green on every hill
makes even dark days light.

SHAKER HEIGHTS, ONE

Some there are
who fly, soar, glide
float, drift, climb
and roll above the clouds
or run about the heavens
        seemingly entitled
as though they were
offsprings of angels.

This presumption is just that,
and yet the angels do conspire
at every love's beginning.
Pumping the wind
as if it were their own to toy with
they die away in ecstasy and exultation
as surely as the poppy petal
or the fragile fruit tree blossom
is finally blown to nothing
by charge after charge
        of clean transparent air.

But is a love only just now
being born
less fragile than a bloom
in its first day of blossoming
swaying on a slender stalk?

Each needs protection,
the coming of other lovers
or the crowded flower bed.

Different every time
and yet containing all
the properties of sameness
love is target
and attracting place
for every element
outside its circle,
jealousy, distortion,
misunderstanding,
and the lack of trust
that distance causes.
Yet I have known some loves
to be so strong
that they can overcome
every element conspiring
to knock them down.

The wind rocks cradles gently
even in the storm.

While in the cradle of our love
if we must share our trust
we can do no better
than to share it with the wind.

AFTER THE RAIN

Last night
the wind stopped
pulling at me
and it rained.

It pattered and played
outside my window
like a child crying
gurgling
talking to himself.

Once on a rainy night
                long past
I opened my eyes
        and saw love
and the rain stopped.

Last night
all the rainy nights
of a lifetime returned
. . . and then you phoned.

MY DOG LIKES ORANGES

My dog likes oranges
but he'll eat apples too.
Like me,
he goes where the smiles go
and I'd as soon lie down
with sleeping bears
as track the does by moonlight.

Don't trouble me
with your conventions,
mine would bore you too.

Straight lines are sometimes
difficult to walk
and good for little more
than proving our sobriety
while on the highway.

I've never heard
the singing of the loon
but I'm told he sings
as pretty as the nightingale.

My dog likes oranges
but he'll eat apples too.

DID YOU KNOW?

The air was bearable to me
only just because I had to breathe
but then you must have known that.

I do not think
I could have stood
the green of green trees
too much longer on my own
—even though I had no way
of knowing what I'd missed
by not sharing with you
what I thought was life
        until you stood my bail
            by being here.

ISLANDER

Thought I have been
        an islander
most all my life,
I could sail
around the world
        on *yes,*
if you once used it,
or hike and even pave
new highways
        and new roads
if you were willing
to alternate with me
the task of being
        pathfinder.

An island
is not just a resting place
a rock of isolation
one is carried to
or goes seeking out
for contemplation
        or to be alone,
it is a fortress for a time
that keeps the islander's mind fresh,
resets, rebuilds his priorities
and helps him learn
the convenience of continents
the importance of not being left alone
or to his own devices.

Still, just now,
I wait upon this island
my odyssey stopped still
not finished yet.

How long should I wait?
Not so long that I become
unwilling to rejoin the world
and take my chances.
How long can I wait?
Until the right chance comes.

How long should I ask
                    that you wait?
Until you feel that chance
has turned to sureness,
as long as it takes
for you to master
north and south
and all the other gadgetry
contained within/without a compass.

We will need whatever help
we both amass apart
            to come together.

SUNSET COLORS, ONE

I love the sunset colors
not just in spring
but every day that God
is kind enough to share with me
his red and orange
                  and yellow,
mixed in rainbows
or solid in the stones
and trees and rooftops
of the world He gave us.

Lately I sleep late
and so I seldom see
the scarlet morning
or the gold behind the trees.
I depend a lot on sunsets
Even when no sunset comes
I fill my head
        with all the sunshine past
and sunsets that I know will come.

Looking in your eyes
I see the sun come
even in the darkness.

Do you know
how much I feel for you
and in what kind of way?
I feel the world for you
and in every kind of way.
I think sometimes that I'll explode,
die or disappear
before I have the chance
to tell you how I feel.

Don't let it be today.

TRACING FOOTSTEPS

What I know of friendly winds
I've learned from being on the sea
        sailing no place
going with the wind
making every harbor home.

I'll show you friendly places now
secret places known to only me.

My toll beach where nobody goes.
A tree, *mon arbre*.
We may even see the wind together.

BOZO

Each of us was cheated.
You won the stallion,
prior to the line-up
at the starting gate,
I took home the mare.

How curious
after such a lengthy time
that we should both still covet
one another's runners.
Perhaps that is the basis
for our long unspoken friendship.

Surely your misfortune
at not taming
that wild stallion
to gallop at your will
up the hill and through
                              the vineyards
of the quiet Villa Roi
is mitigated by the visits,
once a year—
more often once a decade.

I have had to learn
that even Casa Angelo
with all its crooks
and cragged secret passages
is not enough for my spoiled filly
to be lost or found in.
It is, alas,
too close a chomping, stomping ground
for horse and rider to be sharing.

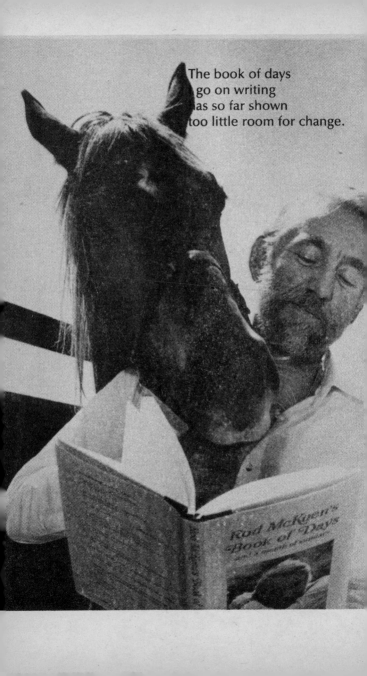

The book of days
go on writing
has so far shown
too little room for change.

But I suspect another book
                of days and nights
is still inside me
waiting to be written.
That means another chance
at life's brass ring
on some aging carousel
in some brilliant new corral.

It is a comfort
that we share the certainty,
                if not the sorrow,
only age can teach;
nothing is so often better than
                                something.

I toast you then
with every grape,
to Venice from
my own backyard.
I know Sebastian's
                    arrows
have not, will not
pin you to the gate.

Hail, kindred spirit
no longer waiting
for the race to start.
All bets are off.

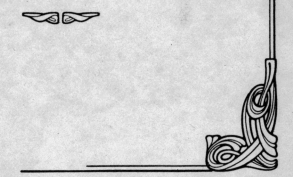

A DAY

I pass by smiling
Aphrodite only shrugs
and looks the other way.
I eye the rain
        and unaware
a rainbow arch takes over.

Void of thought
        and lacking laughter
I am empty
like the summer riverbed.

The road leads north
        as I go south
thinking I let no one
        dictate my direction.
A rabbit, no, a quail
scratches in the bush
and turns all reveries
        to fuzziness.

The river rises
unaware it's taking over
           or does it know,
I wonder which.

Three bells ringing.
I now detect a fourth.
My thoughts are lost
and won't return.

TAKING AIM

Spring began its early reach
             and all of us
went groggy, sleepless
to the docks on Sunday.

Even as we walked
          helloing everybody
the wind of winter
still held on
not fooled by sunshine.

Three days later
we'd be darting
    doorway to doorway
caught by unexpected
        midweek rain.
Winter hadn't left
nor had the spring begun
just because of one long
    sunshine Sunday.

All that spring
and into summer
I was the target
and the aim was true
no one missed me once.

It took so many months
for a single bruise
          to show itself
I might have died
without an outward blemish.
Now the rupture
on the inside
is every bit as true
and tangible
as spitting blood.

Never step into the ring
when the flag is up,
or the flag is waving.
Only when the flag is down.

I wish the rules for everything
were printed in the daily paper,
spelled out on billboards
                ten feet high
or taught to us in school.
Reading, writing, arithmetic
                        and rules
not needed just to pass
the contest or the course
but to get us through
our time allotted here.

The rules and seasons
keep on changing.
I thought at times
my enemies were strangers,
in revolving doors
of my own making
then not strangers anymore.

I suppose they call it
                    target practice
because nobody wants
or needs perfection.

I do.
In the small things.
The sureness of appointments
        and the promise kept.
The knowledge that
I am in control
not always of the circumstance
but surely of the stance,
so that I can traverse clouds
yet one more time.

I'll be back.
Count on it.
I'll come home to you
or if you're gone
              I'll find you.

I feel the need
not just to see you yet again
but to face whatever circumstance
                needs facing.

The firing squad
will find me
waiting unarmed
except for one
small battered
book of rules
I live by.

TRAVEL TIME

Placing my hand
upon your shoulder
and slowly
with my other hand
taking yours to lead you
toward the private heaven
         we've spread out,
we begin to move
to step ahead.
Clocks not wound
schedules left behind,
          we start.

I care not what the populace
cautions or gives warning to.
Kindness I'll return in kind,
because the kindness
              you bring forward
to our once narrow friendship,
              now our so-wide love
spreads with the urgency of fog
and with as much surprise.

Did you know that every hour
each minute given over to me
verifies the way I feel toward you,
more than how you care for me?

Songs you make by smiling,
jigs you dance by lying still,
oceans we cross just by
                looking at them
From the heart's bright windows.

Isn't it a miracle?

JUNE 15

Hurry.
Sunday will not wait,
even for a woman.

The ships are in the harbor
and to catch up now
we'll have to steal
a little time from God
(hard to do with our accounts
                    so overdrawn).

Hurry up.

SUNSET COLORS, TWO

I'll race you up the hill
we can be children
if we want to be.

It's spring
and there's a difference
between children's games and
                    games.

Besides
we're not so old
we cannot still be mystified
                              by marigolds
or dazzled by the dandelion
carpeting the ground
horizon to horizon.

Hurry up
grab my hand
      be careful
but not with me.
Why am I running so fast?
To get there soonest.

I told you once
that I get high
        on sunshine
And you may take that
any way you like.

Be careful
invisible tunneling of moles
has made the ground
            a minefield.

Being Warm Again

For MICHAEL AND ALANA JACKSON

August rainbows make a pastel strip that finally
fades to blue. If you would catch a colored rib-
bon and trace it out across the sky, you should
first know all the puzzle time works out. The
properties of mist, velocity of wind, and whether
sound is bouncing off the satellites and stars, or
you are merely hearing echoes. In every race,
some kind of boundary holds the runner back
and waits along the way. Don't let it stop the re-
lay, but be forewarned.

    Summer winds propel me forward. They al-
ways have. My first groggy Stearman ride a doz-
en years ago on an August Monday morning—six
a.m. and sun up, cured for me all mile-high anx-
iety. What vertigo was left blew past me courtesy
of Art and Art and Dean and Dan and others,
with each balloon ascent in Perris, California.
Later in Black Africa, Ray came and raised us
both a little higher on the scale of life. Though
not Merton's Seven Story Mountain, man's seven
stories of stitched together nylon is worthy of
the wind's attention as God's right hand slips
down to give balloons and the wingless men
who pilot them a gentle prod. When Purvis takes
me bouncing up above the plains of Perth, I'll
add the winds of yet another continent to sky
contacts now piling up.

BOUNDARIES

I love you enough
to let you run
but far too much
to let you fly.

I'll let you walk
the block's end
        by yourself
sail off on any lake
        or silent sea
but if I peer at you
as you go wandering
    through noisy rooms
know that I keep watch
for both of us.

I love you enough
to let you run
but far too much
to let you fly.

THE WILLIAM HARRIS CARD

This is William's card
he passes it out freely
to younger girls and older girls
and housewives in the yard.

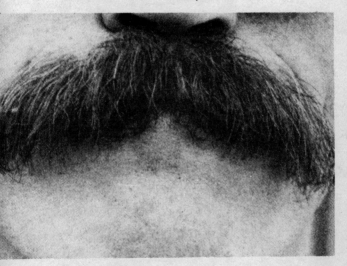

I trust you will
not think of Bill
as being strange or rash
there's more to him than meets the eye
                    or even the moustache.

SANDBAG

Now slowly
like a muffled drum
or the rat-a-tat of rain
the beating of your heart
goes back to steadiness.

Silence separates us
as our pulses slow.
A rivulet and not a ditch
rolls down between us
as though the act
of making love
        has business hours
and five o'clock has finally come.

I know that love
is not red valentines
or flesh on flesh
at pre-set and appointed times
and I believe it to be more
than rhymes and rhyming,
so when I ease to sleep
        against your side
consider my now spent,
sandbag heavy body
as something heart and mind
          let go of
as fodder for a dam
to stop the would be rivulet
        now widening to river
from some oncoming flood.

JUNE FLIGHT

Airborne—free
running with the sun
diving down the day
jumping through June.

Above the world
part of the shell
of some new world.

Now end-over-end
dipping with the down draft
hold on to me—I'm falling.
Catch me if I do.

Or I'll catch you
as no one thought
to reach toward you
              in the past,
airborne in the clouds
or flying stationary
        in each other's arms.
I would not ground you
or terminate your flight
              before its natural end
but I'll be here to catch you
free fall or in a mapped-out,
                        planned
designer's dive.

Why are we here?
Why together—not apart
or each with someone else?
It has to do with more
than love,
that is if more than love exists.
Each of us is here
to buoy each other
keep each other straight ahead
not mixed up inside a mid-June flight
without the sure control
of someone who can offer care
should one of us lose power
over breath or air.

Perhaps then
it is love beyond all thinking
the kind not said
          or put into a letter.

Whatever,
there are no downgrades
on this summer afternoon
only higher, closer fields
                    to play in
not as acrobats or clowns
but as lovers with comedic faces.

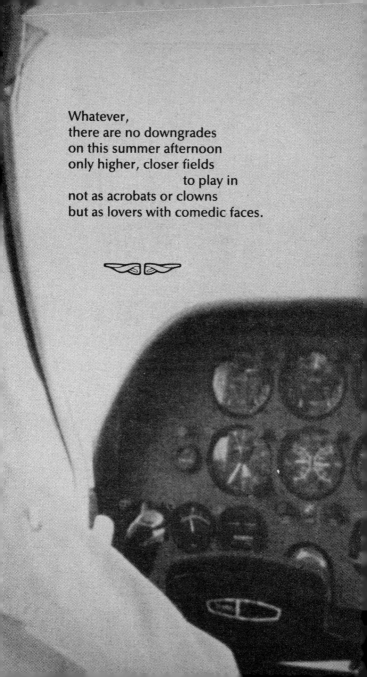

JULY 5

Once I wrote a song
                    almost.
Sixteen lines that walked
up from my belly to my head.

As I stood waiting
for the light to change
and making up a melody,
a yellow bus passed by—slowly.
Looking up I lost the lines
I thought that I had learned
and several more that never came
all because a bus passed by
and someone smiled
from out a yellow window.

Buses pass by seldom
and horsemen not at all
I couldn't crib
or fake your shoulders
if I once forgot
and so each time I hold you
I test myself again.

SHAKER HEIGHTS, 2

The highest angel
turning round and round
will once entangled
plunge toward the dirt.
So earthbound we get twisted
tangled up in hotel sheets
and cloudlike pillows
tumbling like treetop tumblers.

Moving in for comfort,
we cling and crowd
and pull each other outside in
                            inside out
till twins, we roll in circles
to hold each other closer still.

We are each other.
one tight, sustained
and flowing body
wrapped around
whatever core exists
inside or inbetween
the two of us.

I love you and I say it.
I do so yet again aloud.
Not waiting a reply from you,
                    not daring,
I know that on this night
that I could love you
well enough for both of us.

As I know
that none of us
can love enough for two.
It takes a pair of anything
            to make the magnet pull.

What I meant
is that I have the time and need
to wait until you're sure.
Outdistanced only
by the expectation.

Take your time. But hurry.

JULY 12

Don't sit that way.
Your tears fall on your breasts
like raindrops on the window ledge
and I'm reduced to nothing
but a trouble-maker
in a Barcelona chair.
If I want tears
I'll wind the phonograph
and let it do my crying for me.

Women use their tears
              like poison darts.
We're not at war with *love*.
If I've been drafted once again,
I'll pack a bag for Canada.

JULY 15

I have no journeys
that I care to make just now
unless it's to the middle of the bed
(and then I'd own it all).

Where were you last night
                    never mind.
The room is warmer now.

THE SPANISH HILLS

Summer comes late
in the hill country
        trees and grass
both take their time
transforming brown-black earth
                        to green

Bougainvillaea waits
until the middle of July
to climb the walls
and run along each fence.
The Spanish hills are slow
to come awake to summer.

I wish that we
had taken lessons
from the moss and grass
and every Bougainvillaea vine.
If only we had moved
                more slowly
when learning what we learned
                about each other
at west wind, windmill pace.

I wish that we
had taken time to know
the things we shouldn't know
about ourselves.

I shouldn't know
            for instance,
how your sighs come out—
manufactured one by one
till they're no longer sighs
but means of punctuation.

The sun
is on the Spanish hills
I fear we'll not go
                  running there
today again or ever.

What I fear most of all
is knowledge not learned
              at a proper pace,
or experience misrepresented
as truth or even learning.

It is as if a war
was fought without
a meeting of the generals,
the sergeants and lieutenants
                    most concerned
with starting wars
and winning wars.

Or someone started building
seven-story houses
          or an outback shack
without a plan.

If we had paused
somewhere within our
                    headlong run
toward each other's arms
and thought a moment
of the lives
      that we were interrupting,
our own and those about us
we might have had another go
              at climbing up
our so-loved Spanish Hills.

Now even snapshots
or the distant sight
of our own private hills
        against the skyline
will not bring them back.

And so it is our lives
collectively and separately
                are dwarfed.
Not even some low meadowland
gives placidness or permanence
to what we had
in upfront memory
            or some memory bank.

So it is
that separately
we're less than
what we were together.
And at the first
light snow of winter
my mind still circles
like the squawking hawk
around and around
the Spanish hills of summer.

MY FRIEND
AND FIVE STAR FINAL

Frogs croak out
each new edition
as dragonflies supply
the news past noon.

It is left
not only to the morning glory
but field mice in that old
                                fraternity
of sly reporters
filching hill and field alike
to finally flush out all the news.

Better than the radio
                they are
the morning paper
or the grocery handout.

Sometimes I feel
that you invented media
enlisting frogs and dragonflies
as cub reporters and carriers.

The news
comes home to me,
                    good or bad.
Best of all from one
who cares enough
to let me know
of tragedies and triumphs
equal and with love
so I never have to fear
the *Tribune* or *The Times*
reported on the telephone
or at curbside conversation
            by someone else.

In the summer months
your well-paid staff
whispers hard
and tells me all.

Look!
here comes
a dragonfly reporter
                now
his wings so loaded down
with stories to be covered
he stops at nearly every bush
or branch inside the yard
                to rest.

Too late.
There he goes
on wings of wonder
balancing though weighted down.

Never mind
you'll see him later
in the rewrite room
arguing that not a period
            or paragraph
of his now growing tighter prose
                be changed.

How glad I am
that nature nods approval
and becomes your buzzing gossip,
your dandelion digger-up
of in-depth stories
some better left undug,
your bending branch of editor
your wind that sets the type
and holds it there.

I trust
the not-on-deadline
                hummingbird
and bluejay newsboys
more than I have come to know
                and to believe
the columnist or flash reporter
who sits behind electric terminals
and lets machines print out
and process paragraphs of prose
neatly stored and packed away
long before the deadline nears.

The cub
who pokes through ashes
of the fires that smouldered
                    weeks ago
hoping he might find
the human interest anecdotes
to make his story once again
be reinvited to the second page
is stretching facts too far.
I prefer your buzzing bumblebee
                    who pollinates
and then moves on.

But in the backyard—
        this one anyway,
you may tell your caterpillars
and your worker ants
that freedom of the press
and freedom to press on
will always be observed
however criticized
        or reprimanded
the owners of the mortgage are.

THE WINDS OF WAR

The winds of war
no longer hide inside
or thread their way
            through clouds.
Nor do they sit on haunches
at the freeway offramp
waiting to pounce upon
            unlucky strangers
who strayed away
from all the yellow brick roads
meant to lead the traveler
            forever forward.
And the war winds' specialty
of sailing in, then sailing back
and taking with them all the love
stored, piled, and hoarded
by those of us who wished to be
sure that when the famine came
we'd have love to spare, to share
            has ceased to be.

No wind is trickster anymore
except where funnels start
              far off
then turning to tornadoes
carry Dorothy and her shaggy Toto
                 to exotic places.

Wind has learned that love,
while not a conqueror,
wins far more battles
and makes so many lasting treaties
that being in the winner's circle
supercedes the insecurity
that battlegrounds on foreign soil
                    or friendly soil
affords the stumbling, inept soldier.

They go on making and erecting
                      monuments to war
that all the winds
if they were joined together
for a final fatal blow
could not knock down or tumble.

Peace is a wind as evergreen
as everyone would have it.

MID AUGUST

August has been halved.
The warm part done
the cooling just now starting.
If Indian Summer is to be reality
it will congregate at noon
and disappear by five—
barring any miracle
or as yet a plan set out
               but not disclosed.

I light the balcony
           with candles
just before the sun takes leave
sit outside sweatered
in short pants
the phonograph pipes out
long, lean lines
    of nearly bare baroque.
Crickets count out counterpoint
as though rehearsed and listening.

It seems at times
as though each thing
                        that moves
                  upon the earth
or underneath the sky
is trying to communicate,
say something that needs saying.

For now the crickets
seem to dance to music
inaudible, but there.

These ancient dancers
              set the cats
competing for attention.
Distracted by the day's end,
caught up in the night's beginning
I ignore their coaxing
for a snuggle or a scratch,
a chase, a nuzzle or a rub
until they turn to one another
for games too intricate
for so-called human beings.

Quite right,
since something tells us
we are being left out
of something going on
or going, going, gone.
     On this late summer evening
We should be about
the manufacture
              of thoughts
or lack of same.

The cats are making
                   abstract mischief
while I get up
to turn the record over.

THE WAY IT WORKS

Applause on entry.
Now the house is quiet.

The moment chooses me,
demands that I perform in such a way
as to cause ignition or continued silence,
the choice is nearly always mine
sometimes I hesitate, or wait three seconds;
maybe six, too long. The moment goes, is gone.
I will have within that evening
a second or perhaps a third such moment
                              yet another chance.

If I miss each setup,
or hold a note unsteadily
where I should have stopped or paused,
that ovation some had come to give
                    (triggering those who didn't)
will dwindle to polite applause.

It happens.
Lack of concentration,
an eye I should have looked into
or locked upon but didn't or would not
can cause the framework of the evening
to fall forward like a house of bent unsteady cards.

Part of my profession is the taking of risks.
When I am ill prepared, I can't prepare
                              an audience.
Why open up, why come into the ring
                    or circle the arena?
Because somebody has to go and why not me.

Stepping on the stage
is like stepping on the starter,
sometimes you have to pump a while
                    before the engine turns.
(I am sure that there are risks in the business
                              you have chosen
and ones you gladly take.)

And then there is the march,
the banner hoisted high.
Whatever cause that I espouse,
            someone in the middle aisle
or in the bottom bleacher of the crowd
            will be offended.
But long ago I learned a truth:
and in this life but few are given,
that if those people who have followed
and still follow what I do
do not yet understand that one man's freedom,
one woman's hope in jeopardy,
            jeopardizes all of us,
then I invite them, I insist,
they pack up and go home.
They'll find others they can follow
and anyway, I am not a leader,
            I am a *needer* too.

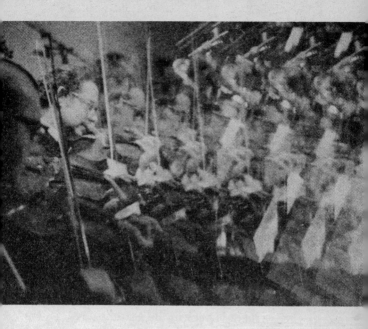

I stay open as a wound
to criticism, but not guilt.
If I join the march or hoist the flag
lend my arms or name, wave the banner
                I do so with consistency.
For every man and every woman
coming down the pike
or floating through the pipeline
in search of freedom
or someone just to hold the candle.

Take advantage of my position,
abuse its privilege you say?
Why the hell do you think
I worked so hard to get here
and plot so hard to stay?
If I cannot give something back
to a nation that affords me everything
then I don't belong.

If I have to take
what some may call the low road
to help a citizen reach higher ground
I'll crawl back in the gutter
once again and proudly.

In case you hadn't noticed,
that's how it sometimes works.

TRAVELING COMPANIONS

Most highways lead away
                       not to
it is the same with roads
and country paths.
Goodbye to what we knew—
hello may never come again.

With suitcase packed
and trunk filled up with nothing,
                       everything we have,
it takes another reticule
to hold the remnants of our past lives
while leaving room enough
to stuff in some remaining bag
whatever trash or treasure
                       lies ahead.

Together
we may go down roads
that seem to have
no sense or sensibility.
But who's to know
what hamlet waiting
            down the trail
will capture our imaginations,
those we thought too old
to be of use,
and make us see
a different side of truth.

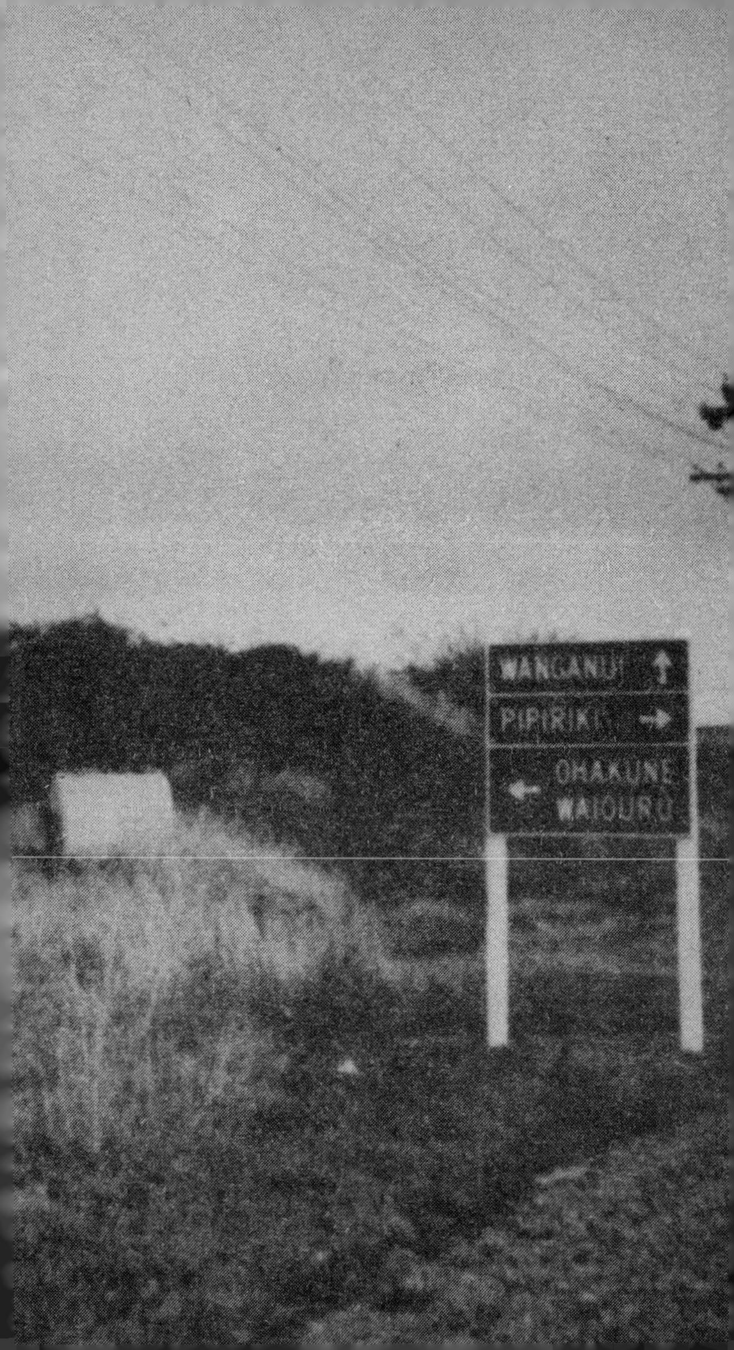
WANGANUI
PIPIRIKI
OHAKUNE
WAIOURU

Together is the word
that conjures magic
and makes Utopia
out of Timbuktu,
changes Alamo into Atlantis.

So it is
that arm in arm
we travel and we tour
we hike down highways
broad and slight
in weather cold
and climate fair.

Turn the corner
turn the page
what you have is THERE.

WELCOME TO TIMARU

INFORMATION CENTRE 7 THE TERRACE

ADVICE TO THE RIVER

River
do not flow
past yourself.
Around the bend
waits more of you.
And nothing more.

JOURNEY

Midsummer
is not the only reason
I am going home
to the yellow corn
and the grasshopper
playing in the tall grass
and the indolent butterfly
darting from marigold
    to rose
        and back again.

I am going home again
to meet the dreaded winter
and the unsure spring.
And the girl whose eyes
                never left mine
when we swam together
            in the river
        and made love
below the old brick bridge.

I am going home to see
if there really is
such a place as home.

It takes a long time
for a single blossom
to fall forward
from a flower tree.
I have so much time to spare
that I can watch
all the flowers fall
from all the trees.

Unprepared for Autumn

For CAROLE BARON

We never learn. Even after several hundred seasons, none of us prepare or are prepared when fall falls into place. It is as though we each expected summer to last beyond the calendar. And when the long and bulging arm of frost reaches out across the land, some of us pretend that autumn is still some miles away . . . a few more kilometers down the road. Why? Because if you're alone in autumn, you'll be alone all winter long.

TELL ME HOW THE WIND BLOWS

Tell me how the wind blows,
and what it takes to find
new waves rolling
down new beaches
and different drummers
    drumming somewhere
       if they do.

Tell me lies,
and if your honesty's a badge
then wear it out of sight.

Especially if you intend
to disavow your love for me.
Save honesty for times
when truth is needed
to make the world four-square
                    and sure.

Make up stories for me
before you turn to leave.
Intrigue me with ideas
to offset your absence.
Cup your hands just so
and tell me, show me
how the wind blows.

SHAKER HEIGHTS, 3

Before you leave for Shaker Heights
I must initiate
a plan for your recapture
without the aid of whiskey—
only that same chemistry
               of need.

Turn before you go
and speak my name again
the way you did
the last time we came through
               the door;
and then I'll know
without another word from you—
               I'll know.

Let me build for you
another mound of pillows
one that you can dive into
                    and hide
from me if necessary
or from the outside world,
that world being anything but me,
                        us.

Now let me tear your pillow building
from its ill-secure foundation
until I find and hold and mouth
                  all parts of you.

The world is white all over.
And like sheets flapping on a line
it blows on aimlessly with us inside.
                    Its destination nowhere.

A CROCK OF FLOWERS

A crock of flowers
on the desk, four days old
begin to die.
No incantations
murmured at their passing.

Left at the roadside
for the garbage man
they become prized
                    widow's weeds,
as one old woman scratches
amid the faded
and still fading castaway
                    bouquet.

She finds three daisies
and a dahlia,
a double sprig of lemon leaves
to brighten for a few more days
an empty coffee can
that decorates a cluttered table.

Even as she walks from sight
she starts arranging
her new floral masterpiece
and passing past a garden
breaks a branch of lilac
to complete her scavengered
                    bouquet.

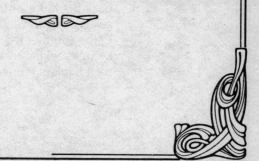

CATS

Cats have the best of it
I suppose they always have.
Curled up in Autumn
back behind the stove,
swaggering through shrubbery
in the summer months.
Pirates seeking treasure
be it hapless mouse or moth.

When ready
for some human contact,
usually at mealtime
or when you're busy
            doing something
they know they can disturb,
they're smarter than the fox
more curious than possums
but they do not extend
            lapdog submission.
A cuddle or a bellyrub
perhaps a scratch behind the ear
                        is quite enough.

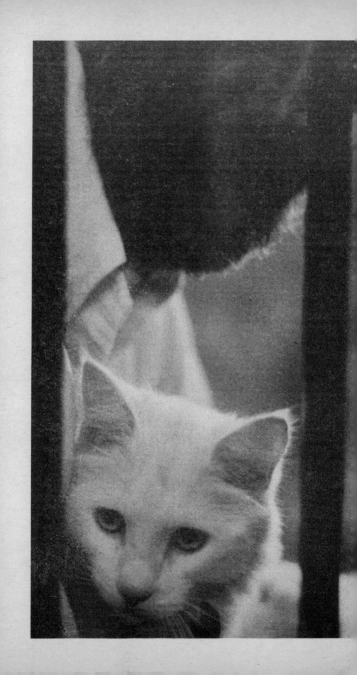

Cats, I reckon, have it all—
admiration and an endless sleep
and company only when they want it.

KNOWING WHEN TO LEAVE

Hello,
I'm here.

I got through one more night
of jacking off and late late shows
                    and sleeping pills
your doctor had prescribed for *you*.

I've arrived again
        to turn your coffee on
and feed your cat
and take your last night's garbage out
and other menial tasks,
like making love to you
before you've had your morning bath.

How like that regiment of men
who've passed down through your life
                    I must be.
You crack the whip
as though you've had a ten-year
                            practice,
barking your commands
like the whispered sighs of love.
I'll never break the chain
though I might rattle it
from time to time.

I wouldn't call my life with you
                            submissive,
it's nothing more than giving back
some of the hope I get from you
                            sometimes
when we're making love
or eating popcorn at the movies
and you smile at me
            and not the pictures.

Still, I'll go softly
when it's time to go
and not wake up
the neighbor's dog downstairs.

I am good at exits.
I leave them laughing
like Durante would.

I never fight back any more,
though that's what we both want,
a fight that proves
how each of us
has wronged the other.

I have learned that when love goes
there is no one you can blame
unless it was The Book of Job
            or Whatshisname.

A NEW LIST OF NECESSITIES

A computer that will store for me
those things my mind is losing.
To have my cake and eat it too
while seemingly refusing.
To fall asleep and wake up
with gargoyles of my choosing.

A WIND

You could feel the rain
before it came,
the signals were that good.

At first the wind
then follow-the-leader
leaves and twigs
until the rain in earnest
smashed them to the ground.

And then your footsteps
slow and steady,
going down the walk, away.

CLOSE

Forward or back
September is the turning time.
Ask the man whose livelihood
                          is apples
or the one who lives for love.

So spreading our arms wide
we gather in September
as a cold man searching
                  after firewood
before the snow
blots out the world.

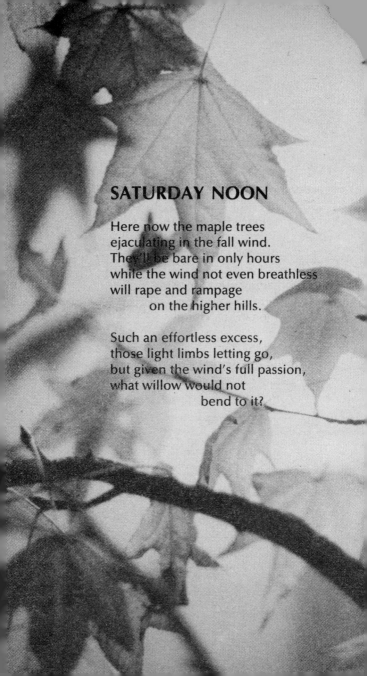

SATURDAY NOON

Here now the maple trees
ejaculating in the fall wind.
They'll be bare in only hours
while the wind not even breathless
will rape and rampage
on the higher hills.

Such an effortless excess,
those light limbs letting go,
but given the wind's full passion,
what willow would not
bend to it?

The pines sweep down
the sky's broad bottom
uninterrupted by the fog
and not bedazzled by the rain,

Each a many-fingered broom
not pretending to be stately
more uncommon or more useful
       than a simple broom.

OCTOBER 15

Nightfall
and on the evening air
comes a lullabye
not for children
but for grown-up people
in love.

Outside the dust lies thick.
The lawns and gutters
are littered with dead leaves.
The night is very long.

TRANSITION

Can you guess what's wrong?
I've tried and failed
to rise above the breakers
to swift sail out the storm.
Now the chance is going
        if not gone.

Will you be the one
to start the argument tonight
or is it my turn, I forget.

I wait here for a sign,
a motion wasted on me.

I cannot say
how long I've waited.
Years pass by within
         a single hour
to those who feel uncared for.

Had there been a signal,
I would have known.

What goes on unseen
untold to us
    by one the other
is more real
than all the sentences
our senses spoke
        and speak.

I see your face and know
a tilting of your shoulder
speaks whole paragraphs aloud
whole stories filled with proof
that what is happening
is if anything a willful lie
both of us indulge in.

This much is fact.
You do not amaze me
with your dark indifference.
You never once astound me
by being only what
          you wish to be.

I await the crumbs just now
delighted that they come
from fresh bread
        lifted out of ovens
by some hidden master baker.

No pride moves ahead
to pave my way.

I've fast become
the dark parts
        of your shadow,
little more than your extension,
hardly more than your left arm.

It tires me to know
I'm just the casing of a window
looking out beyond your world.

After I've packed up
          and gone
fly a flag
should the intruder come.

Take care to give me
fresh reports of all the ships
and all the ducks and seagulls
that sail or waddle beachward.

Be sure to tell me
if the seals come back
             this year
and how the house
gets through the winter.

Keep a diary of sorts
a notebook day to day
that I might thumb through
             or pore over
when I'm living inland
                 miles away.

ROLL OF THE DICE

Will it be remembered
          and by who,
that once upon the blackest
          of Castilian nights
we threw stars,
like diamond dice, along the sand?

And once when it grew quiet
you asked, "Is this love?"
Then before I answered
you had framed and put to me
yet another question.

CHARLES IVES WINTER

It will be a
Charles Ives winter.
You can tell that even now
by the way the branches
       tremble after dark
and the wind rakes up
           the leaves,
saving the rain the trouble.

I've not yet become
an expert on myself
though I thought I was
         a time or two.
But I am willing to drop
my mirror for a while
and hold yours up to you.

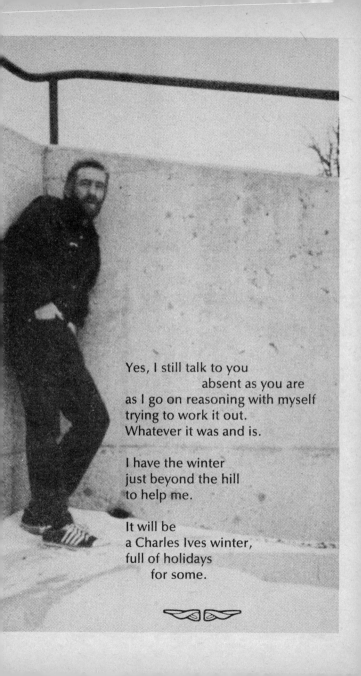

Yes, I still talk to you
                absent as you are
as I go on reasoning with myself
trying to work it out.
Whatever it was and is.

I have the winter
just beyond the hill
to help me.

It will be
a Charles Ives winter,
full of holidays
        for some.

BENEATH THE REEF

the fog
in Laguna this morning
is beautiful.
            you should be here.
i should kiss you from sleep
and
    run
        you
            down
                along the beach
and make you wade in the cool water
your skirts held high above your knees

listening as your laugh is lost
in the sounding of the waves.

I should chase you up the rocks
and catching you
                          hold tight
till my eyes inside
well from happiness
and even out of breath
love should be attempted
on the high rocks
or the white beach
like the love that first
grey afternoon at *Marshall Beach*.

You see
I still plan the day
with you in mind
as though your eyes
were bright for me still
and your head still inclined to mine.

How else could I
attempt to move
through these last August days?

TWO NIGHTS PAST
THE FULL MOON

Finally no one lives here.
Echoes, wind, climate climbing
                    or falling down—
rain rains while no one listens.
In the night, as in the day,
nothing moves, turns, climbs, runs
                    jumps, or even is caught
                          standing still.

Lightning, piercing thunder,
if it does come,
comes someplace else,
and nature's yardstick
has been broken
thus not even quiet
can be measured
            metered out
or put in some perspective
that will finally work
or have some order to it.

People? Where?
None show themselves
not in the morning,
            midnight
or the in-between.
No mouths speak.
No single eye blinks
or closes lazily
against the stars or sun.

Passion seeps
below the bedsprings
to the slats and imperfection
      in the sagging floor.
Truth hides back
behind some bolted door
      that no key fits.
At least not one I own
or loaned to me
and now in my possession.

Not even the legitimate lie,
if there is such a thing
            is bothered with,
trotted out and dusted off
to slide past silence
            into something.

Strangely I'm complacent,
not predisposed or looking.

I believe
and from time's testing
I know it to be so,
that we can look for truth
until all avenues
have been exhausted
and still not find
the measure of it
          that we seek.
Truth seeks us out
if we are open
to the possibilities of what
          that word contains
we should never be afraid
to let it enter in
          and fill us up.

Anxieties that I have lived with
day into night for years,
seem less important now.

This must be some new kind of peace—
            demanding nothing.

What I have done
was done deliberately.
I placed my sensibilities
            in some blind trust
like a presidential candidate
who takes his new influence sincerely.

I do not expect
that one day
        things will change
go back to what we're told
                    is normal.
(And what is normal
certainly one man's definition
            is too simple
as a hundred guardians
of what they call normalcy
confuse, conspire and even
                    trap the word
until it has no meaning.)
There must be reasons
for this unnoticed disappearance
of nearly everything I prized.

Disappointment with myself
        is surely one,
another might be
some new culture
      that crept in
while all our backs were turned.
Indifference,
some new strain
that no vaccine has been
                invented for
must bear responsibility
for so many changes
or so much I cannot figure out.

I only know that even ghosts
would now call this land uninhabited. . .
Do not expect people or a poltergeist
to enter through an archway
or from behind a hidden panel.
Let go
Do not be disappointed.
No keys are jangling
and no door is left ajar.

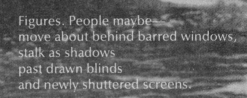

Figures. People maybe—
move about behind barred windows,
stalk as shadows
past drawn blinds
and newly shuttered screens.

Two nights past the last full moon
and all the streets
            are lunar landscapes.

WOOD SMOKE

The geese above the pond
already call out winter
and wood smoke comes
from all the houses
in the town.

We'll move together then
and share the year's last
     warmness
swallowing the rain like brandy.

Tomorrow I'll ask questions.
              Maybe not.
It is enough that winter meetings
happen when the time is right.

No need for talking now
smell the wood smoke
and breathe easy.

PASTORALE

Finally the wind has finished
piling up November leaves.
    Now it turns
to drive the snow in drifts
    along
        the
            fences
of December farms.

The cattle come slow
    or not at all.
They scratch their backs
against the barnyard doors.
Their dialogue,
even as they chew their endless cud,
is low and mournful.

The lazy longhorns,
down the pasture
venture outside only
for a cooling taste of snow.
The wise among them
stay inside the shed
switching tails at what few flies
now survive the early winter.

Lie back.
The wind is on the move
Till the bare tree limbs
stand still again
we've no need to move at all

Turn not away from me
But if you turn toward me
do it in a lazy way
                    and slow.

Let me sleep a minute more.
When the coffee starts to perking,
come to me with smiles.

THE SINGING
OF THE WIND

I stood watching
as you crossed the street
            for the last time.
Trying hard to memorize you.
Knowing it would be important.
The way you walked,
the way you looked back
over your shoulder at me.

Years later I would hear
the singing of the wind
and that day's singing
       would come back,
That time of going
would return to me
every sun-gray day.
April or August
it would be the same
for years to come.

Man has not made
the kind of bromide
that would let me sleep
without your memory
or written erotically enough
to erase the excitement
                 of just your hands.

These long years later
                 it is worse
for I remember what it was
                 even more
than what it might have been.

SHAKER HEIGHTS, 4

Today a letter came.
        No, a card.
The Bijou burned in Shaker Heights
and two adjoining buildings
                fanned the flame.

You must have heard about it.
Perhaps you watched
        from some safe curbing,
new arms around you,
as laddermen in slickers
tried their best to save
                the aging movie house.

Now ocean rolls
beneath my window
every whitecap
like a bursting pillow.

Soon the night
maybe searchlights
or a ship way out.

In the little coves
             this morning
there were pools
of fish trapped,
hands of children
grabbed at them.

Ride a wave for me
           next spring
or run down some foreign beach,
don't forget me.

Make a wish
conjure something for me
kind and capable of caring.

Once wishes were reality—
how fragile is a thought.
It is as if all dreams dry up
or move to other dreamers
    to be taken up
        by them.

ANOTHER TRY
AT TIME ENOUGH

Find me friendly beasts
and I'll lie down
between their legs
easy and with ease.

Show me quiet shores
and I'll run down them
endlessly and without end
till my feet have blisters
from the polished sand.

Give me time enough
and I'll unwind, unset
all the clocks and watches
in the worldly world
so that I'll have time enough
to hike down quiet shores
with friendly beasts.

Should they seek me out
I'll go forward eagerly
with the wildest of the animals,
that friendliest of all the beasts,
             the mind itself.

I often fear
that certain kindnesses
I discern as love
         and caring
are somehow limited,
But even when I feel
      an end approaching
I still hold nothing back.

My greatest guilt in loving
has been the harbouring
         of dark suspicions.
When they are clarified
as nothing more than
gentle ghosts of my imagination
I am still unwilling
to let go of them
or set them in perspective.

I go on believing
space and time are coming,
enough to give me every hour
the new-math need
for adding, multiplying
and dividing emptiness
and dust and ceiling cracks.

No sundial sitting in the shade
is powerful enough
                to rob from me
or hold back even twenty minutes
I feel I have justly been allotted.

Those friends I knew
in Santa Monica,
San Francisco or wherever
all those many years ago
had in common a sense of time.

Time and timing's everything.
Alas, a single minute lost
                is not made up.

Had I waited
but a moment longer
I would still be
on the beach and running
living days of sun
and shell-collecting,
nights of stars that fall
into a metal bucket
and are kept forever
            on the mantel,
if only as reminder that the dreamer
can still pull out packages of light
                        as needed
to help him with his dreams' extension.

2.
I lie here in a quandary.
          Which way now?
Back toward that sea-beach
no longer quite the same,
or hike a higher hill?
                    But where?
Surely there are places
          where both meet.

The beach in Santa Monica
is now some lunar landscape.
Lenny's gone and Aggie too.
Where black sand sloped
and slouched toward the sea
concrete spreads, and cement ends
are tucked in like a blanket.

Perhaps the sun has set
on Santa Monica
forever.

I go there
only out of idleness
or desperation now
or to fill my pockets
full of peanuts at Chez Jay
and talk for hours with him.
Why is it balloons make sense,
                              bi-planes too,
while silver-bellied jets
are nothing more than vehicles
taking time travelers
backwards and forwards
into the future, back to the past?

Wilma's called to say
that she might write a book.
I hope she does,
to clarify it all
to tell us where mistakes were made
and how we might have used
not only Time the runner
but the sun and stars
and certain seashells too
to aid in simplifying not just life
but the living of it
in a jaunty and more joyous way.

Wilma too
has left the oceanside,
moved back up north
and brags of children
growing up and getting tall.
Grandchildren soon, she says.
I listen and I think,
            but not aloud
that even now
I would like to take her half around
the wide Australian coastline—
just to show her beaches still exist
where no footprints mar the sand.
And scavengers go only
to their own familiar places.

We do not speak about Australia
or trouble over California's past
We talk about our children
and she complains of new aches
and impending operations
I tell her I'm more tired
              from this latest tour
than any I've yet taken. Once again
as if to make myself believe it
I say I'm planning to go easier,
slow my gait and stay at home.

Those resolves and good intentions
still find their way by mystery
to the bottom of new lists of words
unfinished or as yet unstarted.

No calls come from San Francisco—
where buildings go on spouting
as if in imitation of Superman's

                        Metropolis,
while in the shadow of grey monoliths
                that pierce the sky,
those seven hundred thousand citizens,
now crowding past a million
wander in confusion, bewildered
forgotten as the forest fauns
while hunters strap the does and stags
to running boards of nineteen-forties

                        pickup trucks
and rusting four-door Buick tops.

3.
Some new cracks
now stretch across the ceiling.
They were not there last week
                             or yesterday
and no new earthquake
rattled at the window
or was reported on the news.

It may be this old house
still finds room and reasons
to go on settling
or is attempting like a friend
to keep my promises intact for me.
In some way I do not yet understand
I think the house now holds
title, trust and ownership of me.

The wind now does its work
within the eaves
more often than it did before.
And even new-tacked shingles
fly into the courtyard
at the slightest breeze.

These are only observations.
No melancholy pulls at me.
I set down only what I notice,
                and I know
that much escapes my eye.

Wind, do your work
and set the weather vane
                    to whirling.
We are friends, not adversaries
and I trust your judgment.
Had I learned that lesson sooner
we might have wrestled time
                        together
and owned our islands
            and our inlets, too.

I will not give up
                 on my belief
that we will yet share life
with one perhaps not known
                              as yet
but coming toward us all the same.

Look up! Look outward!
                 Look around!
Can you not see
something/someone in the distance?

My head is turning slowly now unhurried
like this imagined April day.

I expect that in the year yet coming
I will somewhere, if not here,
once again sleep warm.

INVASION OF PRIVACY

Should you break open
God's great eggs
do not expect
            to find
birds of freedom
        flying forth
in search of time
and room enough
to grow as eagles do.

Expect and then accept
punishment for your crime.

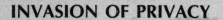

WATCH FOR THE WIND . . . AND WAIT

Watch for the wind . . .
              and wait.
When you see it,
I'll come home.

Listen for the sun
and then be anxious,
when you hear the sun move
through the cottonwoods
and down the hill
I'll not be far behind.

Stop time if you can
         and if you can
then you'll prevent
             my leaving.

About the Author

Rod McKuen was born in Oakland, California, at the tail end of the Depression. He has worked as a lumberjack, miner, salesman, rodeo rider, ditch digger, disc jockey, rodman on a surveying unit and newspaper columnist, among other occupations. Since the mid-nineteen sixties his books have sold in excess of 35 million copies—making him the best-selling and most widely read poet of modern times.

Of the over 2000 McKuen songs (accounting for sales of 200 million plus records), some of the most popular standards include JEAN, IF YOU GO AWAY, SEASONS IN THE SUN, LOVE'S BEEN GOOD TO ME, I THINK OF YOU, THE PORT OF AMSTERDAM, A BOY NAMED CHARLIE BROWN, I'LL CATCH THE SUN, THE WORLD I USED TO KNOW. His film music has twice been nominated for the Academy Award and he is the recipient of numerous Grammy, Emmy, and Golden Globe awards. His classical music, including symphonies, concertos, sonatas, and tone poems, is performed by leading orchestras and soloists around the world. McKuen himself has conducted at Carnegie Hall, London's Royal Albert Hall, The Sydney Opera House, and The Hollywood Bowl. His SUITE FOR ORCHESTRA & NARRATOR: THE CITY was nominated for a Pulitzer Prize in Music.

Rod McKuen's citations and awards include: The Freedoms Foundation Medal of Honor, the Man of the Year Award from the First Amendment Society, the Horatio Alger Award, the Man of the Year Citation from the Menninger Foundation, and the prestigious Carl Sandburg Award as "the people's poet—because he has made poetry a part of so many people's lives."

In 1982, he was named Man of the Year by the Salvation Army and received the American Patriot Medal for his work on behalf of humanitarian causes. His book FINDING MY FATHER not only became a best-seller in scores of countries but also served to initiate new legislation in the field of adoption and adoptees' rights. He works actively for Animal Concern, a foundation established to help preserve vanishing wildlife species and to award scholarships in animal husbandry and veterinary medicine.

In early 1982, the composer/author was named chairman for the National Committee for Prevention of Child Abuse and spent the better part of the year lecturing and working on behalf of child abuse prevention programs. The campaign grew into an international one as Rod became the worldwide spokesperson for this often ignored and censored social issue. It is one particularly close to him personally, as McKuen was himself an abused child—and his first revelations publicly of this previously unrevealed aspect of his childhood made front-page news.

Despite success in so many fields, no one really knows very much about the private Rod McKuen. That may explain the curiosity and anticipation of his long-awaited autobiography which he is currently completing.

While not traveling, for pleasure or on tour, Rod McKuen spends most of his time in a rambling Spanish house in Southern California with his two children and his brother, Edward—and a menagerie of animals he calls "the immediate family."

Sources

Poetry and prose that has not appeared previously in any of the author's books include: SHAKER HEIGHTS 1, 2, 3, & 4, MID AUGUST, BENEATH THE REEF, A CROCK OF FLOWERS, THE WINDS OF WAR, BOZO, SAND-BAG, TRAVELING COMPANIONS, A WIND, THE CONFIRMATION OF COLORS, THE WILLIAM HARRIS CARD, A NEW LIST OF NECESSITIES, INVASION OF PRIVACY, THE RUN TO SUMMER, UNPREPARED FOR AUTUMN, and WINTER ABSENCE/WINTER MEETINGS. In addition, more than two dozen of the poems in this book were extensively rewritten and appear here in their new versions for the first time.

AFTER THE RAIN (aka FEBRUARY 14), OCTOBER 15 are from the author's first book, AND AUTUMN CAME.

TRACING FOOTSTEPS (aka FOUR), JOURNEY (aka NINETEEN), SINGING OF THE WIND (aka EIGHTEEN) are from LISTEN TO THE WARM.

JUNE 15, JULY 15, JULY 12, KNOWING WHEN TO LEAVE (aka AUGUST 27), CHARLES IVES WINTER (aka OCTOBER 14) are from IN SOMEONE'S SHADOW.

MY DOG LIKES ORANGES is from CAUGHT IN THE QUIET.

A WIND and PASTORALE are from FIELDS OF WONDER.

DID YOU KNOW?, TELL ME HOW THE WIND BLOWS, CLOSE, and WOOD SMOKE are from WITH LOVE.

SATURDAY NOON is from MOMENT TO MOMENT.

SUNSET COLORS ONE, SUNSET COLORS TWO, THE SPANISH HILLS, JUNE FLIGHT, WATCH FOR THE WIND . . . AND WAIT are from CELEBRATIONS OF THE HEART.

TRANSITION is taken from the American edition of THE SEA AROUND ME.

TAKING AIM, TRAVEL TIME (aka NAMES . . . with much new material for this edition), MY FRIEND AND FIVE STAR FINAL (with new material for this edition), and ISLANDER (extensively rewritten here) appear in COMING CLOSE TO THE EARTH.

ROLL OF THE DICE, and ADVICE TO THE RIVER are from THE BEAUTIFUL STRANGERS.

ANOTHER TRY AT TIME ENOUGH is from DISTANT BUGLES, approximately nine pages of new material written for this book.

THE WAY IT WORKS is from THE POWER BRIGHT AND SHINING.

CATS is from ROD McKUEN'S BOOK OF DAYS.

A DAY (aka 12–18), BOUNDARIES, TWO NIGHTS PAST THE FULL MOON are from the privately printed quarterly ROD McKUEN'S FOLIO.

Index to First Lines

Photo Credits

Pages 2–3 by Rod McKuen.
Page 8 by Hy Fujita.
Page 10 by Donald Bradburn.
Pages 16–17 by Rod McKuen.
Page 19 by Hy Fujita.
Page 27 by Wayne Massie.
Page 28 by Hy Fujita.
Page 30 by Rod McKuen.
Page 31 by Rod McKuen.
Page 33 by Edward Habib McKuen.
Page 36 by Rod McKuen.
Page 39 by Edward Habib McKuen.
Page 44 courtesy of Australian News Service.
Page 46 by Alan Catt.
Page 48 by Donald Bradburn.
Page 52 by Edward Habib McKuen.
Page 57 by Hy Fujita.
Page 59 by Rod McKuen.
Page 62 by Wayne Massie.
Page 66 by Edward Habib McKuen.
Page 70 by Wayne Massie.
Pages 72–73 by Rod McKuen.
Page 74 by Rod McKuen.
Page 76 by Hy Fujita.
Page 77 courtesy of William Harris.
Pages 78–79 by Fred Neidner.
Page 81 by Hy Fujita.
Page 83 by Rod McKuen.
Page 86 by Rod McKuen.
Page 87 by Rod McKuen.
Pages 88–89 by Wade Alexander.
Page 92 by Rod McKuen.
Page 95 by Hy Fujita.
Page 97 by Bob Lewis.
Page 100 by Rod McKuen.
Page 101 by Hy Fujita.
Pages 102–103 by Rod McKuen.
Page 106 by Rod McKuen.
Page 111 by Hy Fujita.
Pages 114–115 by Hy Fujita.
Page 121 by Rod McKuen.
Page 122 by Rod McKuen.
Page 128 by Hy Fujita.
Page 129 by David Nutter.
Page 131 by Ben Spiegel.
Page 133 by Ben Spiegel.

Page 135 by Ben Spiegel.
Page 137 by Ben Spiegel.
Page 140 by Rod McKuen.
Page 142 by Wade Alexander.
Page 143 by Rod McKuen.
Page 147 by Hy Fujita.
Pages 148–149 by Rod McKuen.
Page 150 by Hy Fujita.
Page 152 by Helen Miljakovic.
Page 155 by Edward Habib McKuen.
Page 158 by Hy Fujita.
Page 160 by Hy Fujita.
Page 161 courtesy of Bob Crewe.
Page 166 by Peter Gottmer.
Page 168 by Wayne Massie.
Page 169 by Hy Fujita.
Page 173 by Rod McKuen.
Page 177 by Wayne Massie.
Pages 182–183 by Edward Habib McKuen.
Pages 184–185 by Rod McKuen.
Pages 188–189 by Rod McKuen.
Page 191 by Rod McKuen.
Page 193 by Rod McKuen.
Pages 196–197 by Rod McKuen.
Page 200 by Rod McKuen.
Page 202 by Hy Fujita.
Page 203 by Rod McKuen.
Page 206 by Rod McKuen.
Page 207 by Rod McKuen.
Page 208 by Wade Alexander.
Page 215 by Rod McKuen.
Page 216 by Wayne Massie.
Page 217 by Wayne Massie.
Page 221 by Alan Catt.
Page 222 by Rod McKuen.
Page 224 by Rod McKuen.
Page 226 by Rod McKuen.
Page 228 by Wayne Massie.
Page 229 by Wayne Massie.
Page 232 by Rod McKuen.
Page 233 by Wayne Massie.
Page 236 by Wayne Massie.
Pages 238–239 by Edward Habib McKuen.
Pages 240–241 by Hy Fujita.
Page 244 by Hy Fujita.